Master Your
Mindset

How To Get What You
Truly Deserve

Mindset Reading

Mindset Reading

Master Your Mindset

Dedicated to
Satguru Mata Sudiksha Ji Maharaj

Thank you for giving me the success mindset.
Finally, with your blessings, I have
finished this book.

Contents

"To change your perspective you have to change your thinking, to change your thinking you have to change your mindset."

— Mindset Reading

Introduction

Everything depends on your mindset. How you feel, think, emotions, and act it's all come under your mindset. It's necessary to have the right mindset in the world where everyone first thinks for themselves.

Nobody cares about you, it's up to you how you prepare yourself to be different from others to not follow the same pattern as everyone else.

A vast majority of people follow the same rules and patterns as everyone else. If you want to do something unique you have to be unique.

You have to think differently you have to act differently. You want to be someone who can also inspire others and motivate others to do the same.

All of these things are possible when you have the right 'Mindset'. Having the right mindset can get you what you truly deserve.

In this book, you will learn and understand how to master your mindset, based on my experience and learning through the years I have put down some tips and understanding about these topics.

This book can help you to grow in your life it can be very helpful if you're In your 20s. Apply the lessons that I've mentioned in this book and understand each concept this can help you to change your mindset and win in life.

Discipline Is The Key

"Discipline is choosing between what you want now and what you want most."

— Abraham Lincoln

I picked this quote because it explains the importance of discipline in our lives. How one should think when you have to choose between the things that you want or the things that you need? There is a big difference between what you want now, and what you want the most.

Discipline is the only thing that can make you go all the way up in your life and become successful. You have noticed that rich people follow a disciplined life even when they have achieved many good things, they know the secret is to do the right thing at the right time and follow the basic rules of discipline.

A man who becomes wealthy through a disciplined lifestyle never flexes. But a man who just bought a luxury item on EMI can be seen flexing with it.

This is why rich people become more wealthy and poor people get poorer every day. They don't understand the difference between what they want now and most importantly what they want the most.

If you understand this concept earlier in your life then you will have a great future ahead.

Now is the time you think about your future goals. And not just think about it, you have to achieve them by living a disciplined life.

Here is a quick self-discipline checklist that you can follow:

1. Read daily.
2. Stay organized.
3. Exercise daily.
4. Focus on priorities.
5. Avoid procrastination.
6. Take a cold shower.
7. Write down your thoughts.

"Small disciplines repeated with consistency every day lead to great achievements gained slowly over time."

— John C. Maxwell

Consistency and discipline are the two pillars If you want to achieve something in your life. When you perform a task daily every day and you develop a practice of it, now you can do that thing consistently. In the book '*Atomic Habits* written by author James Clear, he talked about the psychology of small habits and how they can change your life.

Small habits make a big difference over a period of time when you do it consistently.

My brand '*Mindset Reading*' has around 610k+ followers at the time of writing this book. I build this community of readers just by doing one thing online, Do you know what that one thing is? Just uploading one piece of content every day. Just show up every day and do your part, you will get the results one day.

In my situation I upload content regularly, I do not miss a day, I follow the path of consistency and it gives me the results. Even now it continues to grow, this is the power of doing one thing regularly.

The good thing takes time to show up. Do not limit yourself and go for it. Don't ever think you can't do something, this belief is just in your mind, and it is created by society and our environment.

You have seen and heard many successful people talk about discipline and how it changed their lives. They believe in what is valuable in life and what will give satisfaction.

Do not get confused about what is going around in the world and what is happening on social media, or what is the new trend today. Focus on what matters to you, the things that will teach you valuable skills, which can add some meaning to your life.

Discipline + Mindset

When you want to build a new habit or to start anything new, and you feel like It's very hard to do. That's happened because your mindset is not currently focused on it.

Mindset is very important in every field, anything you are doing if you don't set your mindset to it, you will not be able to do that thing properly. So it's much needed to have a clear goal in your mind and believe that you can achieve that goal.

When you believe that you are going to do it. That's the belief part is called mindset. It's very powerful, it will give you so much of strengths.

When you talk about having a mindset it's not just believing but also having true intention towards your goal. Mindset will not work when you don't truly believe in your goal with intention. You can say It's like manifesting your goals.

It works the same way, but the only difference is, having a disciplined mind and a goal while you have to work for it. You will not just sit and visualize the things to come to you. You have to get up and work for it that's how you achieve your goals.

Master Your Thoughts

"99% of the harm is caused by your head, by you and your thoughts."

— Steven Bartlett

Only you can lead your thoughts and emotions. Don't let anything else control your mind and thoughts.

A man having wisdom knows how to control his emotions. If you know your emotions lead you to perform your actions, throughout the day anything you do, see, or touch these led by your emotions.

Having emotions is good. But letting it control your mind and body it's not good. You can control your emotions this will take some time but you can practice how you can handle your emotions.

Like the above quote which said 99% of the harm is not the actual harm is just the unnecessary thing that you carry through the day it's not real.

You only think this is real harm, but it's not. It causes you problems, It is bad for your body and mind.

If you practice and sit in silence and just observe your emotions and try to connect with them you will realize you can feel those emotions.

This will just take 15min of your day and you will see a big difference in your life.

A Simple Guide to Master Your Emotions.

1. Get up in the morning.
2. Find a silent place to sit.
3. Sit in a meditation mode. (Like monk)
4. Relax completely, and just breathe do not force it.
5. Take a deep breath in and a deep breath out.
6. Perform this for 15min.

While doing this meditation you will have so many thoughts, just observe those thoughts and do your meditation do not think about any thoughts while doing it. In this position, you are just an observer, who will just sit for 15 minutes every day and see their thoughts come and go.

Think like this, imagine you are near a very beautiful river there are so many trees around it, and you sit in one of those trees every day and just see the river but you notice there some moment going on in the water but after some time the moment stops, and the river again becomes silence and still and you continues to watch the beauty of the river.

The *river* is the observer and the '*moment*' is those thoughts that come and go.

You are the observer the thoughts will not stop they will continue to come. You have to train yourself to just be an observer. This is a practical guide meditation you can do every day in the morning. This will help you a lot to master your thoughts and emotions.

Don't be the mercy of your emotions

Now I know emotions are good. It is the necessary thing to feel and enjoy the situation, for example, you need emotions to:

1. Express your happiness.
2. Show that you are angry.
3. Express your gratitude to someone

Show you are in love with something.

You can do and express all the emotions you like based on the emotions or the situation. We are human beings. If we do not show or feel emotions, how can we live? Everything is based on emotions, even though social media nowadays uses technology to control people's emotions to sell their stuff.

How can you save yourself?

Do not let emotions control you. Don't be at the mercy of your emotions. You can use emotions to enjoy them. It is your life; you can control how you live.

"Your emotions are the slaves to your thoughts, and you are the slave to your emotions."

— Elizabeth Gilbert

It is very powerful that one thought can lead to many emotions and it can lead to many outcomes.

You can say, it is like a thread that attached many situations, and each situation can have many outcomes. The outcomes can be bad or it can be good.

It can be anything. But!

If you have learned 'the art of controlling your emotions' then you know that you do not have to do anything.

Everything will be done by itself, you must stand there and only be an observer of the current situation, and see how the situation is handled by itself.

I know it sounds tough and it is hard to do.

It takes a lot of practice to control yourself, especially in situations where you are more likely to lose yourself. That is why people who have achieved and come to the self-control level say, If you want to be a *winning mindset* person then you must practice every day.

Here are 7 things to practice every day

1. Gratitude for what you have.

2. Always be an observer.

3. Try to be an open-minded person.

4. Read a book for 30 minutes every day.

5. Life is a growth. Learn from everything.

6. Sit in silence and meditate every day.

7. Get inspired by other like-minded persons who have achieved success.

Growth Mindset

"To improve is to change, to be perfect is to change often,"

— *Winston Churchill*

In 2017 I was browsing on the internet and got to know the term 'growth mindset'. It was so attractive to me that I ended up researching it all day. I looked up and read every article that I found on the internet, watched every video online, and talked to as many people as I could about this, on the internet.

You can say how passionate I was about the term 'growth mindset'. This is the only reason that I started my brand under the same name

'Mindset Reading' back in 2020. I believe in a growth mindset. I think learning never stops, it does not matter how old you are you can still learn what you want to learn at any stage of your life.

I sometimes look up to my father who is someone more passionate about learning new things than me. I look up to him whenever I feel low and de-motivated in my life. My father is in his 50s; a few months back he told me to teach him how to use a laptop so that he could learn how to create invoices and edit images, and videos for marketing purposes for his business running online.

That is what motivates me to even learn new concepts when I turn in my 50s. I am assuming most of you guys right now are in your 20s or maybe in your 30s.

You have lots of opportunities, train your mind to learn. If you have not built a habit of reading, learning new skills, and getting out of your comfort zone, this is the right time now.

Most of the things you want to learn will be available freely on the internet. One of the reasons that you do not like to learn new things is that your mind currently operates in a fixed mindset zone. You must switch it to a '*growth mindset*'.

If you are new to this fixed mindset and growth mindset concept, let me explain to you how a person thinks compared with both mindsets.

A Person with A Fixed Mindset:

- I am not as smart as this person.
- I cannot do this; it is too hard for me.
- I do not like to be challenged.
- I stick to what I know.
- I do not believe in learning new things.
- I am not good at this.
- I made a mistake.

If you want to become a successful person, do not have a fixed mindset. Most people nowadays you see have this mindset, they do not grow in life. Many people do not want to be around a fixed mindset person.

A Person with A Growth Mindset:

- Every single one is talented.
- I am still learning. I will keep trying.
- I like to challenge myself.
- I like to try new things.
- I am inspired by the success of others.
- I am an open-minded person.
- Mistakes help me learn.

I want to have a growth mindset till I am alive on this earth. You do not know the benefits of having this mindset, above I have just listed down some of the advantages, but if you research about it. You will find many reasons to have a growth mindset. It can help you in many ways.

Many people do not want to change. They enjoy living their current life, with limited things. It is not their problem they just believe that it is their fate. I want to tell you that it is not your fate.

Most successful people have changed their fate from limited belief to having the things that they have dreamt of, but the hard truth is you do not want to do it. The problem is you think you do not deserve it.

Who are you to think that you do not deserve something, if you think that way then first make yourself deserving.

You do not achieve anything if you have a limited mindset. The universe is open to giving you all the things that you need. But it's 'YOU' who have shut all the doors.

"If you shoot for the stars and hit the moon, it's OK. But you've got to shoot for something. A lot of people don't even shoot." - Confucius

A lot of people do not even try something and they want all the things in their life. How is that even possible you must take some action to get something in return.

Don't be in a fear that you will make mistakes without even trying new things. People learn new skills by trying different kinds of things. You must build skills if you want to succeed in life.

This is the reason most people do not even try new things they get afraid of what happen if they fail to succeed. These are all just your inner fear, the fear that you want to fight. So do not think about what happens if:

- You fail.
- You will be criticized.
- Someone judges you.
- You did not learn something.

Instantly switch from fixed to growth mindset

I want to tell you It's all about your mindset. I mean literally If you want to grow in your life and become successful. You should start to switch your mind from fixed to growth mindset. How you can do it?

Here's a practical example to switch your mindset instantly from fixed to growth mindset.

If you fail at something do not ever tell yourself that you have failed. Tell yourself that you do not try your best yet.

If you want to learn public speaking and you decide to speak in front of some people to build your confidence. You go on the stage and you start speaking, and suddenly in the middle, you get blanked. You forget everything that you want to say to the audience. The lecture didn't go well.

In this case don't ever tell yourself that you have failed, or you wouldn't do public speaking again. Make sure you don't use any negative words.

Instead what you should do?

Try to switch your mind instantly and say positive things to yourself like:

- I learned a lot from this.
- I can get feedback from the audience.
- This was an opportunity for me to learn.
- I didn't do my best yet.

The Art of Positive Thinking

"Happiness is not by chance but by choice."

— *Jim Rohn*

If I tell you, your happiness depends on you would you believe me? Well, It's true.

You can choose to be happy right now. No matter what the situation is; It depends on you. You have the choice to be happy in the moment.

Positive thinking happens when you are in a state of happiness. When you feel emotionally good and stable, then positive thinking occurs.

Your mind will always be somewhere else when you need it the most. Thinking positively is the only way you can try to make it work the way you want.

It's you who limits your capabilities

The world itself says I'm possible, why do you limit yourself? You don't want to try to make things happen. The truth is you just want everything to come to you on its own, and you don't want to take any action.

Everyone wants to be happy and successful in their life but the problem is they don't want to work for it. They just want someone else to give it to them.

If you want something you have to work for it. It's the reality. No one will take your responsibility and take your problems. Only you can fight your battle of life, and make change in your life.

Remember our mind holds capabilities that we don't know yet. We can only use it to test how far it can go. So, make things happen with the power of your mind.

Spend time with yourself

The most important thing is to be yourself. When you spend some time with yourself you learn about 'YOU'.

We learn about everything in the world but the one thing we don't learn about is who we are. If we spend some little time with ourselves, we can understand who we are and what we want the most.

The answer is already within us we just don't know yet. Try to go deeper within yourself. You will find peace.

The more you live with yourself you will understand your unique qualities. You get to know your strengths and also your weaknesses. Throughout the day pick a time for yourself, where you will give 30 to 50 minutes to spend with yourself.

Slowly you will realize the power of being yourself. It's important to know your true self.

Live simply, expect little, and give much

One of the best things in life is to make your life so simple. People used to make life hard. Simply put "life is simple we make it hard."

Everything comes under practice. If you want to learn how to make your life simple, you have to practice. You don't have to do a lot of things, just wake up in the morning; and do your regular things. But make sure do not to put any pressure on your mind like:

- Negative thoughts.

- Worry about unnecessary things.
- What to do next.
- Stress to finish anything.
- Achieving a big goal.

Make your life simple for a day and just observe how your life changes. You will notice little things changing in the beginning. But as you practice it every day, big changes start to happen.

The universe will work in your favour when you believe in helping others or giving to others. Don't think about how much you have, you can start by little. You will receive more in the form of many things; It's the power of the universe, this is how it works. The universe will give it to you when you need it the most.

These are the little things that you can practice to be in a positive state. You can look around you will find so many things that can easily distract you.

By practicing these things regularly, you can gain so many of positive things than you can ever imagine.

Focus more on your mind

Your mind is the most powerful tool you have. This is the only reason; they want to manipulate your mind. Our mind is a power machine, it can perform lots of things simultaneously at the same time.

We don't know the capabilities of the mind; we never experienced it. Don't let others feed your mind, be aware of it. Only consume information that you think will be beneficial for you.

This is just the beginning there will be lots of ways, where they try to feed your mind with some garbage. It's up to you how you can save yourself.

Our mind is a tool. It's up to you how to use it.

Now it's the time you make the decision that you no longer let anyone control or manipulate your mind. You have total power and control over your mind. It's you who will decide what to consume or what not to consume.

Be here now, in the moment!

Everyone wants to live in the present. People know being in the present moment feels good. But this is something hard to do. You can be in the present, but for how long?

It's a state of mind where you are alone with yourself. When you are alone with yourself there's no one else. It's just "YOU."

The "*Art of Positive Thinking*" is nothing but being in a state where you emerge with yourself. You are aware of what's happening around you, so you can be very clear when making any decisions.

Surround Yourself with Positive People

"Surround yourself with only people who are going to lift you higher"

— Oprah Winfrey

One of the best decisions of your life would be to choose between with whom you like to spend your time; and what things you are learning from those people.

You must choose people who are going to support you in any situation.

Most people never support each other; people will say they can do anything for their friends. But the reality is different, when the situation arrives the same friend will not show up. This is the harsh reality of today's world.

What is Surrounding?

Surrounding can be your circle, friends, the place where you live, and who you spend most of your time with; these things are so important because these are the pillars of your life.

In the future, your surroundings will decide how successful you become.

Be with good people who have a growth mindset, and people who give positive energy vibes. These are the people who can support you and connect with you more deeply.

The world's most successful people have always been around the people who believe in what they do. Your success depends on who you spend your time with; You also must cut down on people who share negative feelings with you.

Why surrounding is important

The success of any business depends on what relationship you have with the people of the industry.

If you investigate any business or industry the people working there will tell you, it's the mindset of the people that kept them going in the business.

More good relationships = More money

The right surroundings are important because they let you develop the right mindset. If you know the power of how people influence other people's minds with their actions, words, thoughts, and energy, then you can understand the importance of surroundings.

We are the products of our surroundings

Everything you do, speak, or think is not your original concept. We all have been influenced by someone in the past, From childhood we looked up to so many role models that we wanted to become.

Every piece of information has been saved in the subconscious memories of our brain and those data (thoughts, ideas, stories, etc) came out when they needed the most. So in reality most of our thoughts are not actually our own thoughts.

This is why from childhood we should introduce children to reading books. And let children be around a good mentor. A mentor who is well educated about the things that are going on in the present and how we should prepare for the future too.

We are indeed the products of our surroundings and societies.

It's in our own hands we can be good or bad products.

Positive vs negative people

There's a huge role of energy and vibrations of the people with whom you spend your time. If you spend your time with a positive person your mind and body will remain calm throughout the day.

But if you spend your time with a negative person who always talks about negative stuff that goes around in his/her life then you also bring those negative vibrations into your life. So be careful with whom you spend your time.

My suggestion would be to spend your time with a person who lifts you and motivates you when you are feeling low. The person who helps you in your bad times are the ones who are the real ones.

It's hard to find people who carry positive energy within themselves; there's so much negativity going around. If you want to be in a circle of positive people, then first of all you must become a positive person.

Positive energy attracts positive energy.

If you like and want to be in a circle of these people, then you should first become like these people.

Always carry good thoughts and intentions. You would be more likely to meet someone who carries the same energy field.

Everything is your teacher

Surrounding is important, but you can learn from anything in this world if you have a learning mindset. Be curious and ready to accept and learn on the go, take what you need, and move on.

It's up to you what you want to learn. The whole world is your teacher just step outside and see what you like and what you don't like; take what you like and drop what you don't like. It's that simple.

Be a student and open to learning.

Do The Impossible

"You don't have to be great to start, but you have to start to be great."

— Zig Ziglar

We can achieve everything in this world. It is just a mindset of how you see things and your perspective towards it.

Motivation can indeed push you to start the process, but for the long-term game, you have to set your mind to it. Most people don't believe how capable they are; or what things they can do.

You can turn impossible into possible If you just *believe* that you can do it.

What's Impossible?

There's nothing in this world that is impossible. The word itself says I'm possible. We have been programmed from the very beginning to do things that others are doing and say things that others are saying. if you follow this set of rules, then expect outcomes and results for the same.

If you want to break this rule and do the impossible then don't live in the matrix. Break the system and make your own rules. You can be anything and do what you like, you don't have to follow the rules of others; you do what you like to do.

Trust yourself and see what happens. Sometimes you just have to relax your mind and body and see how things change.

You don't always need a plan

Don't fear what will happen if you don't have a plan. No one in this world has a successful plan for their life. Everyone's life is a rollercoaster ride it has lots of ups and downs.

You don't have to figure out all of the things. You just enjoy the ride. Life is more meaningful when you *live* it.

Sometimes you just need to breathe, trust, let go, and see what happens.

This is the same thing I do for myself; when stressed out. When things don't work out, I just simply relax and let go. Some monks follow this technique of '*letting go*' in which they just perform the same thing. Simply relax their body close their eyes and see the magic.

Know your true potential

People who can do some extraordinary things and achieve great success in life are not some different people, they are the same people like you and me.

The only difference is they know their true potential, they have realized what they can achieve in life. You can do the same thing if you know and realize your true potential.

How can you figure out your capabilities?
It doesn't matter what you like or what you don't like. If you want to do the impossible, just set your *mind* to whatever you do.

You decide your own life don't let anyone else tell you what you should do. If you are told by someone else what you should do, you will always be their prisoner. You have to think outside the box. If you want to be on the list of high-achievers.

> *"You are never too old to set another goal*
> *or to dream a new dream."*
> — *Malala Yousafzai*

Change Your Life In 30 Days

"Ideas are cheap, execution is expensive."

— *Shane Perrish*

Practice is everything. In this chapter, we will discuss and learn how you can build any skill in just 30 days.

Learning is the key point of anything you want to start. You first have to gain the knowledge then you can act on that information to apply in your life. This is your first step, In this step get the information as much as possible. You have to learn everything about the skill.

When you gain the knowledge your next step would be to apply.

If you want to build any habit, you should apply the proper knowledge. Without applying you won't be able to learn anything and build any habit.

Consistency plays a big role when you're building any new skill. Without doing it every day you will not grow and learn. You have to do it every day. Consistency is *important.*

In every field not just building any skill or habit. Consistency can be applicable in every area of your life. This is how our brain works, when we do something repeatedly our brain knows and learns accordingly.

It will not work if you just practice for one or two days and then you decide to drop it.

You have to do it regularly. Sends signals to your mind that you want to learn this thing. If you do it every day your brain will remember.

These are the main steps of building any skill or habit that will change your life:

1) Learning

2) Practice

3) Apply

4) Consistency

Learning anything and building any new skill isn't hard, you just have to follow the right system. Follow the right set of rules then you see the results.

The 30-for-30 approach

Let's learn the real method everyone can use to build and learn any habit and change their life in just 30 days if do it the right way. I learned this approach from a creator named *'Sahil Bloom'* I follow this approach to learn any new skill that I want to build.

The 30-for-30 approach is perfect in my opinion because you have to just give your 30 minutes every day for 30 days. This is the straight and simple ideology of this approach.

If you simply take out just 30 minutes of your day. You could build a habit that you have always wanted to build. Remember consistency plays a big role in this, not just doing it for a few days. You have to do it straight for 30 days.

Intensity + Consistency = Progress

You going to see the results when you focus mentally and physically. Most people can't keep up the consistency that's why they never learned anything in their life.

You are not like anyone else; you are the person who takes full responsibility and does the work consistently.

Everyone wants to see the results fast, but only a few are going to wait and bring the results.

Small things become big things.

Progress is a slow process. You are not going to see the results fast. Patience is important.

When you start to learn you progress slowly. This process of doing it for 30 days will become a big thing on the 30th day. You are going to see a big difference. Compare yourself to the first day when you don't know anything about the skill. And now how far you have come.

This is the magic of compounding. If you have read the book '*Atomic Habit*' by *James Clear* he talks about the same concept of becoming 1% every day.

This 1% looks small in the beginning but in the long run, this will convert into a big thing. It's like a snowball effect. The results will show up and you will be surprised.

Your Mindset Determines Your Future

"The people who are crazy enough to think they can change the world are the ones who do."

— Steve Jobs

Your success depends on your mindset. Our mind is the most powerful asset we have. It doesn't matter how many successful people you have met or how educated you are. Your future will be created by how you *think.*

By using your mind the right way, you can unlock the secrets of the millionaire mindset.

If you want to grow and make your future, there is so much information available on the internet. But if you don't know which information to use, and if this information is correct or not. How will you identify? That's where the right mindset comes in.

You are brainwashed from the day you were born.

You have been programmed since you were a child. when you are like 5 or 6 years old you are told and fed with so much information from your school teachers, your culture, society, culture, TV, and media. You also get programmed by your parents because they also have been programmed through their parents.

It's a cycle of manipulation, you can also call this a well-structured system, and we are all a part of it; the difference is we don't know it.

We don't know what's happening around us if you want to get out of it. You have to be aware of what's going on in the world.

Most people who are now wealthy know the system and they are aware of what's the next thing coming.

You have to be prepared for everything. That's how you can break the cycle of manipulation. you are just a product of the wealthiest and they use you for their benefit. When you know and understand this then it will be easy for you to break the system of the manipulation.

No one can manipulate a person with a strong and right mindset.

The right mindset is your real asset, with the use of this you can become whatever you want.

"Success is not an accident, success is a choice."

-Stephen Curry

Don't be a sheep and follow the crowd!

If you want to be successful, don't be a sheep and follow the crowd. You must find out your way of thinking so that you can be different from the rest.

You can't make any changes or progress unless you do things differently from the crowd. Everyone has their unique way of doing things.

Every individual is somehow unique, but we all follow the same line from the start. This is why we forget our true potential. But you are not like everyone else, you are reading this book, and you have ways to be different; and get out of this wrong crowd.

Your circle is important. If you are surrounded by people who have the same energy and mindset then your future will be great.

Most people don't have a way to change their lives, so they just follow the same line blindly and go nowhere else.

But you have decided to not follow the crowd. You are ready to change your mindset.

Be your own unique and individual self.

Don't forget your true self. You are very smart and unique. This happens when you figure out your personality.

When I was in college, I had a group of cool people; we were always in a group. Everywhere we went we went in a group, Sooner or later I realized I didn't have an identity of myself. Who am I? What's my identity here in my college?

So, I decide to make a small circle with only 2 or 3 people. When I was in that small circle for a few months. I noticed my view of things changed, my perspective to look at things started changing and you also started to communicate things deeply.

Group = Weak

Individual = Strong

A group makes you weak. When you are in a group, you don't have any identity. You will always do things from someone else opinion.

Don't discuss people discuss ideas!

Most people nowadays don't know what they should focus on to grow in life. They talk about the success of other people.

How someone else has achieved these milestones in this short time or how much money someone had made at this age.

People don't want to discuss ideas; they don't want to think about how they can also do the same and achieve great success in life.

You can get everything you want if you set your mind to it. Focus on your mind. Believe in what you do and think.

Master Your Mindset

You have so many things to do, you should never waste your time thinking and discussing other people's success.

You Can Get Everything You Want

"Believe you can and you are halfway there!"

— Theodore Roosevelt

Have you ever wondered, what these big celebrities, business persons, millionaires, and billionaires have in common?

They all will say that they once dreamt of all these successes. If you look at any of their interviews they will talk about having a dream or a desire.

Why?

Because, if you want to be anything or achieve any big goal in your life, having a desire is one of the first steps toward achieving that goal.

Desire is the starting point of anything.

It builds into your mind through your thoughts, thinking, and visualization. Everyone has so many thoughts throughout the day.

A strong intention is important while having any desire. Intention is like a powerful *emotion* that works behind a desire.

Thoughts will come and go but it's your intention who hold one of those thoughts and convert it into a desire.

First, you have to decide what you want in life. Based on that goal you have to think of it every day. Imagine yourself having that goal; this imagination process should not be fake. See yourself in mind that you have achieved that goal with emotions and intentions.

This is so powerful if done the right way. Everyday take out just 5 minutes of your day and do this exercise and believe me this will change your life.

The process of visualization and manifestation

How you can start with visualization. Don't make it too complicated. Close your eyes, and start seeing yourself. See yourself smiling. You can be anything in your imagination.

This is like a movie. It's up to you how you want your movie to be. You're the director, you can make it look bad or good.

When you can do this visualization technique well with full intention and emotions, now you can manifest things.

You can get everything you want with the help of manifestation.

I have achieved many things using manifestation. If you don't believe in manifestation you won't be able to manifest things. There's a popular book in Law of Attraction called 'The Secret' The book is written by *Rhonda Byrne*. I'm going to explain in short what the book is all about.

The book talks about 3 steps to manifest things. The first step in the book was to *Ask.*

The very first step is asking the universe what you want. It could be anything just ask with real intentions.

The second step is to believe. In this step, you have to believe that you're going to get your desired thing. Believe in the process of the universe.

The last step is to receive. This is the step where you're going to receive what you have wanted.

This is the 3 step process introduced by the author *Rhonda Byrne.*

If you noticed, this process also talks about believing in what you have desired and that you're going to receive it.

One of the most important parts of manifestation is to take action.

Taking action is always necessary to achieve your goals

If you have done all of the 3 steps mentioned above then just sit down to wait you will not receive any results.

You have to take action. Without taking any action you will not be attracted towards your desired things. In manifestation, a little action is always necessary to achieve your goal.

Many people make the mistake of not taking any action, they just sit and wait for the universe to manifest things for them; This will never happen you have to do some work to attract and then the universe will help you to achieve your goal.

If you want to attract money, you have to think like a businessman. Just thinking like rich people can make many changes in your life. Your mind will work and function differently, and in some days you will notice you have slowly attracted to money.

"The mind is everything. What you think you become."

-Buddha

How it's connected to the universe

When you think or have some ideas on your mind and you have strong intentions about it. Then your thought must have been sent to the universe.

The universe is the creator in the manifesting world, you can ask anything to the universe and you'll receive it.

Whatever you desire will be manifested by the universe, so you've to be careful what to ask about. You have to match your vibrations with the universe so it can understand what you've desired.

This is so amazing that these powerful forces are united together to get your desired thoughts manifested and come to life.

Our thoughts and beliefs shape our reality. So that means you have to make sure of what your thoughts are, and how your thoughts are being created.

Your reality will be made from your thoughts.

Find Your Purpose!

"The mystery of human existence lies not in just staying alive, but in finding something to live for."

— *Fyodor Dostoyevsky*

Nobody wants a boring life. Everyone wants to be happy and alive. This can only happen if you have a purpose in life.

Living a meaningful life is more fun compared to a life where you don't enjoy what you're doing.

Finding your purpose in life is like you born again and now your new journey begins.

Your Purpose = New Beginning

Every single person in this world has a purpose in their life. Most of the people don't know what's their purpose. They live a clueless life and blame their unhappiness on someone else.

Everyone should have a purpose

My purpose in life is learning and teaching others how to live a better life. You can also figure out your purpose. Don't pressure yourself to find your purpose in life.

Simply just live your life. Do whatever you're doing right now, If you are not happy doing it, you have a choice to leave that behind and start something new.

Don't stop searching unless you find something that makes you happy. It could be anything any work, idea, weird job, or something else. Everyone should have a purpose in their life so that they can be happy as long as they live.

Your life would be meaningless without a purpose in your life. If I don't learn anything new or don't write it down to teach others, on that day I will feel like I haven't done anything.

The meaning of life is to find your gift. The purpose of life is to give it away.

-Pablo Picasso

There's a beautiful Japanese concept called *'Ikigai'* This concept helps people find their purpose and live a meaningful life.

It's a perfectly studied concept that has helped millions to discover what truly matters to them and live a joyful life.

This book with the same name 'Ikigai" which was written by the authors Francesc Miralles and Hector Garcia talks about four simple steps to finding your purpose in life:

1) Do what you love

2) Do what you're good at

3) Do what the world needs

4) Do what you can be rewarded for

These simple four steps can be very helpful for anyone who wants to discover their reason for being. If you follow these four steps you will discover your reason for being here in the world.

Doing what you love and in which you are good is not that hard. Doing something you love is a signal that you already enjoy doing it.

But It could be something that the world is not ready for or the world doesn't need it. You have to make sure that your purpose is something that the world needs and you can be rewarded for it.

You may be only a few steps away from finding your purpose. It's not that hard to figure it out. Maybe you're currently living a meaningful life and you don't know yet.

Books Can Change Lives

Books can be dangerous. The best ones should be labeled "This could change your life."

-Helen Exley

One right book at the right time can change your life forever. Books are one of the best sources for educating yourself.

I have been reading books for the past 8 years. I started reading books as a hobby and now I have a huge library in my home.

Most of the books are non-fiction books but I remember my first book was fiction, can you believe it?

It just happened that I liked reading nonfiction after that; because I used to consume information on personal development. So I started searching for books related to that only and read most of the popular books that we see online.

If you want to change your life completely, start reading books.

Life is a continuous growth, A book is a source of regular growth in life. If you are not reading you're not growing. Every successful person will advise you to read more books.

Reading is not just for information. There's a reason why avid readers tell you to read books. When you start reading books you develop your own thinking. You develop your mental models which will help you to be creative when necessary.

Bring a book with you everywhere you go

One of the best habits you can build when you want to read books is to bring your book with you everywhere you go. Reading can be done anywhere in the world. If you're not an avid reader this is the best advice for you to take your book with you.

This is the best way to build, a habit of reading every day. I suggest everyone read at least once a day; this will help you be accountable for your reading habits. Habits a built when you perform a particular thing consistently.

Building a reading habit is one of the best things you can do. You will thank me later if this advice helps you in any way.

My process of reading books is simple. I don't want to make things complicated. Allocate your time in a way that you fully relax on that time so that your brain can work correctly.

And you observed everything you read. It is the most important thing to reflect on what you have read.

Find your unique taste in books!

This is one of the best advice for beginners. If you want to build a reading habit you should find your taste in reading. You have to find a category in books that you like reading it could be biography, business, productivity, spirituality, romance or science.

The category could be anything, the main point of having a taste is to be consistent in reading. Once you build a habit of reding every day you would automatically read other niche's that is the power of reading books.

A book can influence you in so many ways. I started reading books in the motivation niche, and slowly I explored many niches in books.

This is how you know yourself. You didn't know what you ended up liking once you started reading.

Many people in their 20s asked me how they can develop reading habits daily. They want to be consistent with reading. I tell them to first know your interests and what they like doing besides reading.

If you have a habit that you like doing every day then you can pick up a book with the same interest there are lots of books available online.

Let's say you like doing fitness you do exercise every day. Then you can find a book on "how to have a lean body in 30 days." This way you will not get bored reading. Because now you like doing exercises and now you're reading about it and gaining some knowledge of it.

Knowing your interests will keep you in touch with reading, even when you stop reading for some days.

"Read what you love until you love to read"

-Naval Ravikant

Naval Ravikant is the biggest inspiration for me and many others who need wisdom, knowledge, and some modern philosophy.

In the process of reading and figuring out your taste in books, you will discover your love for reading. Once you start reading books there's no going back. You will start finding new books and you'll build your library.

Why read physical books?

You can choose whatever format you like to read. But I like to read physical books paperbacks and hardbacks. Most people prefer digital devices for reading. Everyone has their comfort for reading, some people also prefer audiobooks.

Audiobooks are great when you're traveling and also when you're working at home or cooking. It's a good habit to listen to books while you're busy with other work. You can simultaneously do both works.

I have always been a fan of physical books. When I started reading books the first book I bought was a paperback. I like the pleasure of flipping the pages. I like the smell of a new book page, the cover of the book, and the texture, I like everything about physical copies.

This is just one of the reasons I prefer to read physical books. There are many reasons to read physical books:

1) They can help you sleep better

2) The chances of distraction are less

3) You can consume more information

4) Your eye health will improve

5) Physical books have health benefits

6) Your screen time will decrease

Physical books have always been a motivation for me to buy and read more books. When I buy a book I like to wait for the book to deliver to me. That excitement of waiting for your book to arrive is another level of pleasure.

The importance of re-reading books

It's not remarkable to read 100 books. But to read 10 best books a hundred times. When you read a book one time you get some clarity but when you re-read the same book you get a deeper level of understanding.

Because our mind works that way when we read again and again we get introduced to new things our brain connects so many thoughts on the same piece of information that we read in the book.

I have a habit of reading multiple books at the same time. Most of the time when I like a particular book I drop other books to read the one book which I like the most.

By doing this I know what I am reading and what I'm interested to read so that I can re-read the same book again for more in-depth knowledge.

Books are the ocean of knowledge. There are plenty of books you can choose from, you can discover what you want to read based on your mood and feelings.

My quality of thoughts changes when I re-read a good book. It's a lot about analysis, understanding, patience, and enjoyment while re-reading. I suggest you read it again and again when you don't get the core message of the book.

What's the point of reading a book when you don't completely understand the writer's core message? You can learn so many things from a single book.

While re-reading a book you can get other ideas also; this happens when you get yourself into the flow state.

Flow state is a meditative stage where you are so involved in a particular activity that you don't focus on anything else while you're doing it.

It's ok to drop a book in the middle

You don't have to finish a book. If you don't like it you can drop the book in the middle of reading. Most readers have this pressure of finishing every book they read. It's not necessary to finish a book.

It's your choice to drop a book if you no longer feel connected to it. When you buy a particular book now that book is yours, you can write in it, draw on the page, and make notes too.

You can start reading a book in the middle also, it's up to you how you want to learn from the book.

I sometimes start books from the middle if I like a specific chapter it doesn't matter to me everything is fair in reading and learning.

Don't feel the pressure of completing every book you own. Give yourself time and read what you like. You are not a machine you're a human being you have a choice you can pick your book and what you want to learn based on your mood and situation.

Feel free to read anything. The most important thing is you want to grow yourself, growth never stops. There's learning in anything you have a learning mindset.

Read both fiction and non-fiction

My first book was a fiction book that I read when I was 19 years old. I honestly liked that book, I enjoyed every part of it—the story of the book, characters, scenes, and writing.

You can learn and improve yourself by reading both fiction and non-fiction books. I have learned so many things reading fiction books however I like reading non-fiction they are my favourite. But I want to explore fiction books too.

I have a curiosity to read different genres of fiction books so I can compare and understand more in-depth the writing of these types of books. Fiction can give you so many things at the same time.

You should have a purpose for reading when you pick a book. If a person shares a book of their choice It's because they like that book. It doesn't matter that you are also going to like it.

Without a clear vision or a goal in reading, you can read so many unnecessary things. You have to have a goal in mind, what you want to read, and what you're going to achieve from reading.

Non-fiction books are great for self-development no doubt. It's your choice what you prefer reading and what you like.

Taking notes is important!

There's no benefit of reading when you don't take notes. If you don't take notes, how would you reflect on what you have read?

Reading a book is one thing but taking notes is another thing—when you read a whole chapter from the book you can summarise the entire chapter in a paragraph as notes.

You can consume those notes anywhere you want you don't have to carry the book you can simply open your notes and read.

Taking notes excises your brain to work better and improves your thinking abilities—because when you take notes you write in your own words, this forces your brain to function better and enhances your thinking capabilities.

I write my notes in my separate notebook. Everyone has their style of taking notes from the book. Some people write in the book itself and that's also a good way of taking notes.

I prefer my little notebook to write. You can use all these notes in the future to help others or you can publish your notes as a book. It's a very good idea to write a book with the help of your notes.

Many authors do that—famous author Ryan Holiday uses this technique to write his books. He uses a system called "*The Notecard System*" a very popular system that you can use to store your information in a categorized way. You can divide each of your information by topic.

Read out of curiosity

Reading is one of the best things that happened in my life. When I was in college I used to hate reading. I don't know how I suddenly liked reading It happened accidently.

Although I had the curiosity to know things since childhood, maybe I found books as a medium to know more about different things that I'm curious about.

This is the best medium to know more about what you're interested in, you should have a curiosity to explore and find information about a particular thing that excites you.

You can find hundreds of years of knowledge written in books, how fascinating is this—and you can pass on this knowledge to anyone who wants to know about it.

Watching videos and reading books to consume information is a whole different thing. I prefer reading over watching videos.

When you read, you're not only reading your mind is focused on the book. You're also not distracted by anything. You're so involved in the reading. I would always go for reading over watching videos for consuming information that I like.

21 Life Lessons I Learned in My Twenties

"Your twenties matter. Eighty percent of life's most defining moments take place by the age of thirty-five." – Meg Jay

1. Your family is most important

Your family comes first. You need to keep in mind that if you're facing any problem—there will be your family who will always support you. And stand beside you in any situation.

2. Time is the most valuable thing

Everyone has 24 hours only so it's up to you how you use this time. Some spend their time learning some skill and some waste this time scrolling on social media.

This time will never come, so be careful and use your time wisely and effectively.

3. Know the power of listening

Most people don't ever listen. Communication is the best way to make new friends and It also builds your confidence. Don't listen to just reply, listen to reflect on it, think about it, and then reply.

4. Choose your friends wisely

Friends can make you or break you. Don't make too many friends, have a small circle.

Your friends should be real, not fake ones. They should uplift you, motivate you, and support you for your passion.

5. Stop comparing yourself to others

You're unique, don't compare yourself to any-one else in this world. Everyone in this world has a unique personality. You are 'YOU.'

Know yourself, find your true potential, and then see how much you can achieve in this world. You don't know your capabilities yet.

6. Build a side hustle

If you're in your 20's then focus on building a side hustle. This is one of the best things to do, trust me you'll thank me later.

You can figure out online how to start a side business in any niche. If you're confident about the niche, then start your side hustle.

7. Believe in what you are doing

You must believe in yourself when you believe in something your half work is done. Only be-lieving makes it possible.

Anything you can do If you just believe.

8. Don't spend on materialistic things

If you want to become successful, don't chase materialistic things—you can make your 20s worse by doing this.

Materialistic things are just a short dopamine for a short period. You must control yourself in your 20s.

9. Know what you are consuming online

The Internet is freedom. You can consume whatever you like. But you also must realize this can harm you if you aren't aware of what you're consuming. You can take good things and drop bad things from the internet.

10. Focus on building skills

Skills are the future in any industry you see. If you have a particular skill you can survive in the future. You must focus on building skills.

11. Life is what you make it

It's totally in your own hands, how you want your life to look like. Your decisions matter a lot, you're thinking matters a lot, and how you do things and take actions matters a lot.

12. Build a habit of reading books

If you learn some things early in life, it stays with you forever. Reading habit is one of the best things you can build early in your 20s.

If you're not a regular reader, just think about it and start reading books every day—it will change your life.

13. Always have good intentions

Positive people attract positive people. If your intentions are good you will always be everyone's favourite person.

Make sure to have good feelings and intentions for people around you.

14. Update yourself with the current trends of the world!

You must be up to date on what's happening around you. Have an open mindset to think and understand about the trends around you.

Update yourself as the world changes every day.

15. Focus on building wealth

Wealth is real freedom. If you focus on building wealth you'll never be broke in the future. It gives you complete freedom to do what you want to do.

16. Spend more time making big decisions

Your life's progress depends on which decisions you have taken. Don't make big decisions with emotions.

Think about every aspect when making a decision that going to change your life.

17. Write down your thoughts

Writing down your thoughts is like therapy. Make a habit of writing down every morning, and keep a small journal for your thoughts.

18. Listen to what your elders say

When we're growing up in our 20s, we think that we know everything about the world. But the reality is we don't know anything about the world.

So please listen to elders carefully what they're teaching you about the world, relationships, friendships, money, life, and the list goes on.

19. Learning from your past and making better choices

Life is a learning game. You never stop learning. Nobody cares when you make mistakes in your 20s.

You have a chance to learn from your past and make your future better.

20. Life is a movie, you're playing a lead role

If you think closely, you'll realize life is a movie and you're the main character. And our whole life from start to end is directed by God.

21. Everything is meaningless in the end.

No matter what you have achieved in your life, in the end, you're going to die, this is the reality of life.

Everyone's going to die in the end. Be happy and grateful for everything that you have.

The Art of Focus

"What you focus on grows, what you think about expands, and what you dwell upon determines your destiny." — Robin Sharma

What is the focus? And most importantly how to focus on the things which we wanted to do. These are the questions on everybody's mind.

It's not an easy thing to focus on your most important task. I've been there when I wanted to focus on some things I always got distracted by many things.

There are systems, some tips, and guidance to follow to fully concentrate and do your work with focus.

Nowadays this is very important to train your mind to do a 30-minute focus meditation. This will calm your mind to concentrate more on your tasks. Meditation is something that will help you not just focus but many other helpful things in your life.

Increasing focus is one of the best benefits of meditation. You can immediately feel the calmness in your mind and relaxation in your body.

I've been doing this for almost 3 years. I can say meditation is the secret to increasing your focus. My routine is to do 30 minutes of breathing exercises and some yoga poses to complete my stretching exercises.

If you have never done these breathing exercises then you should try this and see the change in your mind, body, and spirit.

Social media/phones steal your focus.

You have to be careful how you use your phone and social media these days. The biggest thing that I am also scared about is the algorithm of the apps, which are designed in a way that pretty much steals your focus every time you use your phone.

These big tech giants don't care about your mind. They just want to brainwash you so that you can use their apps all the time and they make money out of it. This is the harsh reality of the big tech giants in the world.

We use their apps every day and we also give our data to these tech companies so they use this huge data to know your interests what you like, what you don't like how you react to a post, and what is emotions when you look at a picture on their app. They know about you everything.

Based on this huge data they use their algorithm to show you the same information on your phone so they can manipulate you. This is scary. They control you they control your emotions, your mind, and your thoughts.

How you can save yourself

First, you have to be aware of what's happening. When you are fully aware of their intentions then it will become easy for you to tackle this problem.

You have to understand what's their aim and what they want to achieve by manipulating the audience.

When you know their intentions then you can avoid and identify the information which they want to feed you on these apps.

Many people are brainwashed every day after consuming certain content on social media.

The Internet can be good or it can be bad, depending on how you use it.

Train your mind to filter out the content and know the difference between such information that they want you to consume.

Our mind is designed to focus.

It's because of some social media and phone distractions we're not able to focus as we used to be.

Phone distraction is something we all have to take care of; put your phone in another room when you're doing your important work.

You can also put your phone on silent mode when you want to do the intense work.

We all face this issue of notifications and sound alerts from our phones every day. It's in our own hands how we use our phones.

We can limit ourselves to using the phone or delete all the apps that steal our focus every day through their notification sounds. It's very important to have a plan to tackle this thing.

Phone distraction also decreases our productivity, and because of this, we aren't able to perform our favourite tasks with full concentration.

You can able to do your actual work when you have a proper system to avoid phone distractions.

20 Tiny Habits That Will Change Your Life

"Habits are the compound interest of self-improvement" - James Clear

1. Master the art of listening

If you want to have a great conversation you first have to master your listening skills. Listening is so important in communication.

If we're not listening actively, we can't understand the next person.

2. Read two pages a day

Reading can be one of the best habits anyone can build. Reading every day has many benefits.

3. Do at least one activity outside

Make sure you do at least one activity outside your home. Be in nature's fresh air and some have sunlight on your face.

4. Master a skill that you like

If you're good at any skill you must master that skill so that it can benefit you in the future.

The future is for those who have built some skills.

5. Get up early in the morning

Early mornings could be a great start for your work. Your productivity level will be on pick in the morning.

6. Reduce your screen time

Keep your phone in silent mode or out of your reach for some time in the day. It will reduce your screen time and give your eyes a little bit of rest.

7. Get enough of sleep in the night

For your mind and body to fully function in the morning you have to get at least 8 hours of sleep.

Forget everything a good night's sleep should be your highest priority.

8. Make a to-do list for your everyday tasks

Organizing your everyday tasks could be life-changing for you. Make your to-do list so that you will be clear about your everyday goals.

It will also increase your productivity to do more in less time.

9. Breathe through your nose

Nose breathing could be very helpful for your body. It will decrease your stress level every time you deep breath through your nose.

10. Gratitude every morning

Make a habit of gratitude every day. Be grateful for what you have. It will keep you down to earth and you'll be always in a happy mood.

11. Invest in yourself

Investing time, energy, and money in yourself will be a good decision you can make.

You'll not regret it. It will give you a chance to grow yourself more and learn.

12. Make your bed

One of the best habits you can make. It will set your mindset throughout the day if you just make your bed.

13. Drink enough water throughout the day.

Water intake throughout the day can help you boost your mood and keep you hydrated the whole day.

It'll also make your skin look good.

14. Learn to be alone

If you do not have a good company with yourself then you're doing something wrong. Spend some time with yourself, you'll understand your true self more deeply.

15. Take 1-2 minute cold shower

If you want to feel alive. Just take a cold shower every day for 2 minutes. It will boost your mind and body instantly. This can change your life.

16. Have a positive mindset

A positive mindset can help you grow in life. The right mindset can lead you to success.

17. Don't always be available for everyone

Your time is valuable. Make your time useful, don't be available for anyone or anytime. People are used to taking advantage.

Make time for people who care, listen to you, give their time, and respect you.

18. Master 80/20 principle

80% of your results are coming from 20% of your hard work. This rule can apply to anything.

19. Write down your goals

Write down what you want to achieve. Knowing your goals and writing them down makes it a little bit easier to get closer to them.

20. Be happy from the inside

You should be happy genuinely. A happy person attracts more positive people.

Master Communication Skills

"To effectively communicate, we must realize that we are all different in the way we perceive the world and use this understanding as a guide to our communication with others."

– Tony Robbins

Communication has become a very important skill nowadays. If you do not know how to properly communicate with someone, you will not be able to express yourself fully.

I think perfect communication happens when you truly engage with the conversation. and authenticity.

Most people think a great conversation is about the language we are using. But it is not true. What makes a great conversion? It is a mixture of a couple of things: eye contact, smile, being interested, being fully present, and body language.

So even when you're talking in your native language and you are aware of these little things you can perfectly turn a boring conversation into a good one.

When you are in your twenties you can learn communication skills very fast. Your mind is ready to experiment with new things, so even if you haven't spoken a new language before you can easily learn it.

One of the best things I have discovered about communication is that if you are interested in the topic or the person you are talking to then it becomes so easy for you to lead the conversation.

"You can make more friends in two months by becoming interested in other people then you can in two years by trying to get other people interested in you."

– Dale Carnegie

In his book "How to Win Friends and Influence People" Dale Carnegie talked about becoming genuinely interested in people. You can easily make more friends in two months by being genuinely interested in people, and you can only do this when you let go of your ego.

A couple of years ago I was an introvert. I didn't want to talk to people for more than a minute. I was not confident enough to show people that I liked talking to them. This happens a lot when you are a close-minded person. Now I'm trying to improve myself and I can say I have come a long way and find myself more comfortable when I'm around people. This one lesson can help you a lot to become better at communication.

So if you're in your twenties make sure you practice every day on your communication. The future is all about skills. If you have built some skills you'll face very less competition in your field. Sometimes I just talk to people to sharpen my communication, to see how I sound, and to test my confidence level. I was a Hindi medium student. I still cannot believe I am writing this book.

You definitely can do anything if you set your mind to it, your mind holds a tremendous amount of possibilities. You just don't know what you're capable of doing unless you try to do it. If you just start and believe in yourself you possibly can achieve anything in your life.

The Importance of Listening

*"When people talk, listen completely.
Most people never listen." — Ernest Hemingway*

In a world bustling with noise and distractions, the art of truly listening has become a rare and valuable skill. As humans, we often fall into the trap of waiting for our turn to speak, instead of genuinely hearing what the other person is saying.

When we intentionally listen to someone, we not only hear the words being spoken but also pay attention to the underlying emotions, intentions, and messages conveyed by the speaker. When we listen attentively, we gain a deeper understanding of the speaker's thoughts, feelings, and perspectives.

So, if you want to have a genuine conversation. Make sure you truly listen to the person what he or she's saying and carefully try to connect with the person deeply, then It'll be very easy for you to communicate with the person.

Listening with empathy allows us to step into the shoes of the speaker and understand their experiences and emotions. This helps build trust and strengthens the bond between individuals, leading to more meaningful and authentic connections. When we genuinely listen to others, we signal that we value their opinions and perspectives. This helps build trust and rapport, as individuals feel heard and respected.

7 Tips to Be A Better Listener

1. Listen with an open mind.
2. Make eye contact with the person.
3. Don't focus on the person, focus on what is being said.
4. Ask questions when you don't understand something.
5. First, listen closely to the person, don't just be ready to reply.
6. Be in a good body posture, while sitting or standing.
7. Make sure you are genuinely interested in what is being said.

Read these seven tips again and again, when you remember every tip now is the time for you to implement these tips in your conversation. Don't just read and forget about it, tips and advice will do nothing if you don't act or apply them in your daily life.

Why You Should Communicate with Confidence

Communicating confidently is a crucial skill that can positively impact our personal and professional lives. When we express ourselves confidently, we convey our ideas effectively, build trust with others, and inspire them to believe in our abilities.

Communicating with confidence means having faith in our thoughts, opinions, and abilities to express them. It allows us to share our ideas, contribute to discussions, and engage with others in a meaningful way. Confident communication helps us establish credibility, showcase our expertise, and create positive impressions.

Confidence enables us to articulate our thoughts and ideas clearly and concisely. When we communicate clearly, we increase our chances of being understood and respected by others. Confidence in communication helps establish trust and credibility.

When we speak with assurance, others perceive us as knowledgeable and trustworthy, which enhances our personal and professional relationships.

4 Practical Exercises to Improve Confidence

Exercise 1: Do Mirror Practice

Stand in front of a mirror and practice delivering a short speech or presentation. Pay attention to your body language, tone of voice, and facial expressions. Visualize yourself speaking with confidence and purpose. This exercise helps build self-assurance and improves overall presentation skills.

Exercise 2: Practice Role-Playing

Engage in role-playing scenarios with a friend or family member. Take turns playing different communication roles, such as expressing opinions, delivering feedback, or handling challenging conversations.

Exercise 3: Positive Affirmations

Create a list of positive affirmations related to confident communication, such as "I am a clear and effective communicator" or "I speak with confidence and conviction." Repeat these affirmations daily, especially before important communication situations.

Exercise 4: Challenge Yourself for Speaking

Seek out opportunities to speak up in group settings or public forums. Offer your thoughts, ask questions, and actively participate in discussions. By challenging yourself to contribute regularly, you build confidence in expressing your ideas and engaging with others.

7 Brutal Truths About Life

"You'll literally never know what you want to be when you grow up" – Sahil Bloom

1. Life is not predictable

Even if you give your 100% effort, follow all the rules, do everything right, and still you can fail.

Anything can happen in life you just can't predict.

2. Prepare yourself first

You have to be prepared for life. The world doesn't give a sh!t about you and nobody cares. Be on your own, learn, and grow.

3. Choose your friends wisely

Be careful when you choose with whom you want to hang out and spend your time.

Sometimes your best friends can leave you when you need them the most.

4. Money and success is not the end goal

Most people think having lots of money and becoming successful is the ultimate goal of life.

When the reality is different, money is good but it's not the end goal. Having freedom is the goal—freedom from society, thoughts, matrix, manipulation, and freedom from everything.

5. In the end you'll left with nothing

This is something I think of every time. All the money you've earned, fame, family, memories, good people everything will be gone when you're no longer here.

This is the ultimate truth.

6. You're not perfect in anything

You'll never achieve the highest level of perfectionism—no one can achieve it.

It's just about learning and growing, perfectionism doesn't exist.

7. Talent is nothing, practice is everything

You can learn anything if you invest your time and energy in it. It's about practice and how many hours you've put into that work.

Consistency, and showing up every day can lead you to success.

Mindset Reading

Other Books by Mindset Reading

100 Lessons To Learn In Your 20s

100 Lessons That Will Change Your Mindset

Don't look at anyone else do not compare yourself to anyone else

Embrace your own Body Shape

Find a style that works for you body + shape.

Join the community!

Visit mindsetreading.com to learn more.

Instagram: @mindsetreading

Twitter: @mindsetreading

Everyone is them
You are you.
Embrace Please embrace
your Body be
proud of it
anywhere you need to
make changes make
tem
Buy new Bra if that
helps / change you
scral like you are
here Im so proud
of you.
Once you get use
to trying new
ways you will be
napper

I love my Athletic
sporty Body
~~Bys~~ Bike riding
Football.
Netball
Now Badminton
Go Go Go Go
No one ~~#~~ will come
in my way.
I Exept me whole
heatdley / You
will look good if you
appreciate your own
Body your own
personalthe
Your personalty is
UNIQUE ITS
YOU

My Body
Exept Except and love the
Shape and size of my
Body.
Be thank-ful and
grateful for having
Such a beautiful
body.
Do not ever compare
you beautiful body to
anyone else's
Embrace You
Sporty
Fun.

tall
Happy
Sports look.
Interesting look
You are you that's
the best part

~~Et anyone else~~ can ge
~~OPINION~~